# Mastering Email Subject Lines: Unlocking the Secret to High Open Rates

Roy Hendershot

Published by Roy Hendershot, 2024.

MASTERING EMAIL SUBJECT LINES: UNLOCKING THE SECRET TO HIGH OPEN RATES

**First edition. June 8, 2024.**

Written by Roy Hendershot.

# Table of Contents

Mastering Email Subject Lines: Unlocking the Secret to High Open Rate......... 1

Chapter 1: Understanding the Basics ........................................................... 3

Chapter 2: The Psychology Behind Subject Lines....................................... 5

Chapter 3: Crafting Your Perfect Subject Line............................................ 7

Chapter 4: Personalization and Targeting.................................................... 9

Chapter 5: Testing and Analyzing Subject Lines ...................................... 11

Chapter 6: Subject Lines for Different Types of Emails........................... 13

Chapter 7: Overcoming Common Challenges ........................................... 15

Chapter 8: Leveraging Data and Trends..................................................... 17

Chapter 9: Advanced Techniques and Strategies....................................... 19

Chapter 10: Building a Sustainable Strategy.............................................. 21

Chapter 11: Automation and Tools for Efficiency .................................... 23

Chapter 12: Industry-Specific Strategies .................................................... 25

Chapter 13: The Future of Email Subject Lines......................................... 27

# Introduction: The Power of the Perfect Subject Line

Every email you send has one chance to make a first impression, and that chance is the subject line. Imagine walking into a bookstore. You see a shelf full of books, each one with a cover trying to grab your attention. Some are flashy, some are simple, but only a few make you curious enough to pick them up. Your email's subject line is like that book cover. It's the first thing people see, and it decides whether they'll open your email or ignore it.

You might be wondering why the subject line is so crucial. It's just a few words, after all. But those few words hold incredible power. They can make someone stop what they're doing and click on your email, or they can make your email blend into the sea of unread messages. A great subject line can boost your open rates, which means more people will see what you have to say. Whether you're promoting a product, sharing a story, or sending a newsletter, a compelling subject line is your ticket to being heard.

In this book, we're going to dive deep into the world of email subject lines. We'll explore why they matter, how to craft them, and the secrets behind their success. We'll look at real-life examples, uncover the psychology that makes them work, and learn how to test and analyze them. By the end of our journey, you'll have the tools and knowledge to create subject lines that not only get noticed but get opened.

We'll start by understanding the basics. We'll look at what makes a subject line effective and why it's an essential part of your email strategy. Then, we'll explore the psychology behind subject lines. You'll learn how human behavior influences email opens and how to use this knowledge to your advantage. We'll also cover practical tips for crafting the perfect subject line, including personalization and targeting techniques.

But we won't stop there. Testing and analyzing your subject lines is crucial for continuous improvement, so we'll dive into A/B testing and other methods to see what works best. Different types of emails require different approaches, so we'll discuss how to tailor your subject lines for promotional, transactional, and informational emails. We'll also address common challenges and how to overcome them, such as avoiding spam filters and staying creative.

Data and trends play a significant role in shaping your strategy, so we'll look at how to leverage these to stay ahead of the curve. Advanced techniques like using humor, storytelling, and multimedia will help you stand out even more. Finally, we'll build a sustainable strategy that keeps your audience engaged over time.

As we embark on this journey, remember that mastering email subject lines isn't just about getting more opens. It's about connecting with your audience in a meaningful way. It's about making sure your message gets the attention it deserves. So, let's get started and unlock the secrets to high open rates and effective communication.

# Chapter 1: Understanding the Basics

———

Before we dive into the nitty-gritty of crafting the perfect subject line, let's start with the basics. What exactly is a subject line, and why is it so important? A subject line is the text you see in your email inbox before you open the email. It's the headline of your email, and it's there to grab your attention and make you want to read more. Think of it as the hook in a story or the tagline of a movie. It's meant to pique your interest and draw you in.

You might think that a subject line is just a tiny part of your email, but it's actually one of the most critical elements. Why? Because it's the first thing people see, and it often determines whether they'll open your email or not. In a crowded inbox, where people receive dozens or even hundreds of emails every day, a compelling subject line can make all the difference.

So, what makes a good subject line? There are a few key characteristics that effective subject lines share. First and foremost, they are clear and concise. People don't have time to read lengthy or confusing subject lines. They want to know at a glance what the email is about. A good subject line gets to the point quickly and clearly.

Another essential quality of a good subject line is that it sparks curiosity. It gives just enough information to make the reader want to know more, but not so much that they feel like they already know what the email contains. It's a fine balance between being informative and intriguing. For example, instead of saying, "Our Summer Sale Starts Now," you might say, "Don't Miss Our Biggest Sale of the Summer!"

Subject lines also need to be relevant to the recipient. This means understanding your audience and what interests them. A subject line that works for one group of people might not work for another. This is why it's crucial to know your audience and tailor your subject lines to their needs and preferences.

Another aspect to consider is the tone of your subject line. The tone should match the content of your email and your brand's voice. If your brand is playful and fun, your subject lines should reflect that. If your brand is more serious and professional, your subject lines should align with that tone. Consistency is key.

It's also important to avoid certain pitfalls when crafting subject lines. For instance, using all caps or excessive punctuation can come across as spammy and may turn people off. Similarly, misleading subject lines that promise something the email doesn't deliver can damage your credibility and lead to lower open rates in the future. Honesty and transparency go a long way in building trust with your audience.

Understanding the basics of subject lines is the foundation of effective email marketing. As we move forward, we'll delve deeper into the psychology behind subject lines, explore practical techniques for crafting them, and learn how to test and analyze their performance. But first, let's take a closer look at the psychology that makes subject lines work.

# Chapter 2: The Psychology Behind Subject Lines

---

Now that we've covered the basics, let's dig into the fascinating world of psychology and how it influences email subject lines. Understanding the human mind can give you a significant advantage in crafting subject lines that resonate with your audience and compel them to open your emails.

One of the most powerful psychological principles at play in subject lines is curiosity. Humans are naturally curious creatures. When we encounter something intriguing or mysterious, our brains crave more information. This is why subject lines that spark curiosity can be so effective. A well-crafted subject line can create a sense of intrigue, making the reader want to open the email to satisfy their curiosity. For example, a subject line like "You Won't Believe What Happened Next" piques interest and encourages the reader to find out more.

Another key psychological principle is urgency. People are more likely to take action when they feel a sense of urgency. This is why subject lines that create a sense of urgency can be incredibly effective. Phrases like "Limited Time Offer" or "Act Now Before It's Too Late" can prompt readers to open your email right away. The fear of missing out, often referred to as FOMO, is a powerful motivator.

Emotional triggers also play a significant role in subject line effectiveness. Emotions drive behavior, and subject lines that tap into emotions can be very compelling. Whether it's excitement, joy, fear, or nostalgia, evoking emotions in your subject lines can increase the likelihood of your email being opened. For instance, a subject line like "Relive the Best Moments of Your Childhood" can evoke nostalgia and prompt the reader to open the email.

The choice of words in your subject line is crucial. Certain words have the power to elicit strong reactions and drive engagement. For example, words like "exclusive," "free," and "new" can grab attention and encourage opens. Additionally, action-oriented words like "discover," "learn," and "unlock" can create a sense of anticipation and excitement.

Social proof is another powerful psychological principle that can influence subject lines. People tend to follow the actions of others, especially when they are uncertain. Subject lines that highlight popularity or social validation can leverage this principle. For example, a subject line like "Join Thousands of Happy Customers" can create a sense of trust and encourage the reader to open the email.

The psychology of scarcity is also worth considering. When something is perceived as scarce or in limited supply, it becomes more desirable. Subject lines that emphasize scarcity can drive urgency and prompt action. For example, "Only 3 Spots Left" or "Limited Edition Available Now" can create a sense of exclusivity and urgency.

Understanding these psychological principles can help you craft subject lines that resonate with your audience on a deeper level. It's about tapping into the natural human tendencies that drive behavior and using them to your advantage. As we move forward, we'll explore practical techniques for crafting subject lines that incorporate these psychological insights.

But before we get to the nuts and bolts of writing compelling subject lines, let's take a closer look at some real-world examples of subject lines that successfully leverage these psychological principles. By analyzing what works and why, we can gain valuable insights to apply to our own email marketing efforts.

# Chapter 3: Crafting Your Perfect Subject Line

Armed with an understanding of the psychology behind subject lines, it's time to put that knowledge into practice. Crafting the perfect subject line involves a combination of art and science. It's about finding the right balance between being informative, intriguing, and relevant to your audience.

The first step in crafting a great subject line is to be clear and concise. Your subject line should convey the main message of your email in as few words as possible. People are busy and don't have time to read long-winded subject lines. Aim for a subject line that is around 50 characters or less. This ensures that it will be fully visible on most devices and email clients.

Next, focus on creating a sense of curiosity. Your subject line should give just enough information to make the reader want to know more. It's about teasing the content of your email without giving everything away. For example, instead of saying "Our New Product Line Is Here," you could say "Discover Our Exciting New Product Line."

Personalization is another powerful tool in your subject line arsenal. People are more likely to open emails that feel tailored to them. Using the recipient's name in the subject line is a simple but effective way to personalize your emails. For example, "John, Here's a Special Offer Just for You" can grab attention and make the reader feel valued.

In addition to personalization, targeting your subject lines to specific segments of your audience can increase their effectiveness. Different groups of people have different interests and preferences, so it's important to tailor your subject lines accordingly. For instance, if you're sending an email to a segment of customers who have previously purchased a particular product, you might say, "Exclusive Deal on Your Favorite Product."

Crafting a compelling subject line also involves using action-oriented language. Words that encourage the reader to take action can increase open rates. Verbs like "discover," "learn," "unlock," and "explore" create a sense of anticipation and excitement. For example, "Unlock the Secrets to Better Health" is more engaging than "Health Tips Inside."

Avoiding certain pitfalls is just as important as using the right techniques. For example, steer clear of using all caps or excessive punctuation, as this can make your email look spammy and unprofessional. Similarly, avoid using misleading subject lines that don't accurately reflect the content of your email. This can damage your credibility and lead to lower open rates in the long run.

Testing your subject lines is crucial for continuous improvement. A/B testing allows you to compare different subject lines and see which one performs better. This involves sending two versions of an email with different subject lines to a small segment of your audience and then analyzing the results. The subject line with the higher open rate is the winner and can be used for the rest of your audience.

Crafting the perfect subject line is an ongoing process. It requires creativity, experimentation, and a deep understanding of your audience. By applying the principles we've discussed and continually testing and refining your approach, you can create subject lines that not only get noticed but get opened.

Now that we have a solid understanding of how to craft compelling subject lines, let's explore how to personalize and target your subject lines for even greater impact. Personalization and targeting can take your email marketing to the next level, helping you connect with your audience in a more meaningful way.

# Chapter 4: Personalization and Targeting

———

Personalization and targeting are powerful strategies that can significantly boost the effectiveness of your email subject lines. When done correctly, they make your emails feel more relevant and tailored to the recipient, increasing the likelihood of them being opened.

Personalization goes beyond just using the recipient's name in the subject line, although that's a great start. It involves using any information you have about the recipient to make the email more relevant to them. This could include their past purchase history, browsing behavior, or preferences. For example, if you know that a customer recently purchased a camera from your store, you could send an email with a subject line like "Jane, Enhance Your Photography with These Accessories."

Segmenting your audience is a crucial step in personalization. By dividing your audience into smaller groups based on specific criteria, you can tailor your subject lines to each segment's interests and needs. Common segmentation criteria include demographics, purchase history, engagement level, and geographic location. For example, you might have a segment of customers who frequently purchase sports equipment. A subject line like "Special Offers on Your Favorite Sports Gear" would likely resonate well with this group.

Timing is another important factor in personalization. Sending your emails at the right time can increase their relevance and impact. For instance, if you know that a customer often shops on weekends, sending an email with a subject line like "Weekend Exclusive: 20% Off Just for You" could encourage them to make a purchase. Additionally, considering time zones and local events can help you choose the optimal time to send your emails.

Dynamic content is a powerful tool for personalization. This involves using variable data fields to insert personalized content into your subject lines and email body. For example, if you're running a promotion on different products in different regions, you could use dynamic content to create subject lines like

"Exclusive Sale on Winter Coats in Your Area" or "Summer Essentials Now on Sale Near You."

Personalization also extends to the tone and style of your subject lines. Understanding your audience's preferences and communication style can help you craft subject lines that resonate with them. For example, if your audience is younger and more tech-savvy, you might use a casual and playful tone. On the other hand, if your audience is more professional, a formal and straightforward tone might be more appropriate.

Testing and analyzing the effectiveness of your personalized subject lines is crucial for continuous improvement. A/B testing different personalized elements can help you understand what resonates best with your audience. For example, you could test using the recipient's name in the subject line versus not using it, or test different personalized offers. Analyzing the results will provide insights into what works best for your audience.

While personalization can significantly enhance the effectiveness of your subject lines, it's important to use it wisely. Over-personalization or using data in a way that feels intrusive can have the opposite effect. It's essential to strike a balance between making your emails feel relevant and respecting your audience's privacy.

Now that we've explored the power of personalization and targeting, let's move on to testing and analyzing your subject lines. Testing is a critical part of the process, allowing you to understand what works best and continually refine your approach. In the next chapter, we'll delve into the techniques and tools you can use to test and analyze your subject lines for optimal performance.

# Chapter 5: Testing and Analyzing Subject Lines

---

To truly master the art of crafting email subject lines, it's essential to test and analyze them. Testing helps you understand what resonates with your audience, while analysis allows you to refine your approach for even better results. This chapter will guide you through the process of testing and analyzing your subject lines to ensure they're as effective as possible.

The first step in testing your subject lines is to set up A/B tests. A/B testing, also known as split testing, involves creating two versions of an email with different subject lines and sending them to a small segment of your audience. By comparing the open rates of the two versions, you can determine which subject line performs better. The winning subject line can then be sent to the rest of your audience.

When setting up A/B tests, it's important to test only one variable at a time. This means that the two subject lines should differ by only one element, such as the wording, length, or use of personalization. Testing multiple variables at once can make it difficult to determine which factor influenced the results. For example, you might test a subject line with a sense of urgency ("Last Chance to Save 20%") against a subject line that sparks curiosity ("Our Biggest Sale of the Year").

Once you've conducted your A/B tests, it's time to analyze the results. The primary metric to look at is the open rate, which tells you the percentage of recipients who opened your email. A higher open rate indicates a more effective subject line. However, open rate isn't the only metric to consider. Click-through rate (CTR) and conversion rate can also provide valuable insights into how well your subject line engaged your audience and prompted them to take action.

In addition to A/B testing, you can use multivariate testing to test multiple variations of a subject line simultaneously. This approach allows you to test different combinations of elements, such as wording, length, and personalization, to see which combination performs best. Multivariate testing can be more complex than A/B testing, but it can provide deeper insights into what drives your audience's behavior.

Another valuable tool for analyzing subject line performance is heat mapping. Heat maps visually represent how recipients interact with your emails, showing which areas receive the most attention. While heat mapping is typically used for email body content, it can also provide insights into how well your subject lines are performing. For example, a heat map might show that recipients are more likely to open emails with certain words or phrases in the subject line.

Tracking trends over time is also important for understanding subject line performance. By analyzing the performance of your subject lines over weeks, months, or even years, you can identify patterns and trends that can inform your future strategy. For example, you might notice that subject lines with a sense of urgency perform better during certain times of the year, such as the holiday season.

In addition to quantitative analysis, qualitative feedback can provide valuable insights into your subject line performance. Asking your audience for feedback on your emails, including the subject lines, can help you understand what they like and dislike. This feedback can inform your future subject line strategy and help you create more engaging and effective emails.

Continuous improvement is the key to mastering email subject lines. By regularly testing and analyzing your subject lines, you can stay ahead of the curve and ensure that your emails consistently perform well. Remember, what works today might not work tomorrow, so it's essential to keep experimenting and refining your approach.

With a solid understanding of how to test and analyze your subject lines, you're well-equipped to create subject lines that get noticed and get opened. Next, we'll explore how to tailor your subject lines for different types of emails. Different emails require different approaches, and understanding these nuances can help you craft subject lines that resonate with your audience in every situation.

# Chapter 6: Subject Lines for Different Types of Emails

———

Email marketing isn't a one-size-fits-all approach, and the same goes for subject lines. Different types of emails require different strategies to ensure your subject lines are effective. In this chapter, we'll explore how to tailor your subject lines for promotional, transactional, and informational emails, as well as for seasonal and event-based emails.

Promotional emails are designed to promote a product, service, or offer. The goal is to entice the recipient to take action, such as making a purchase or signing up for a webinar. For promotional emails, your subject line should create a sense of urgency or highlight a compelling offer. For example, "Limited Time Offer: 50% Off All Items" or "Hurry! Sale Ends Tonight." The key is to make the recipient feel that they need to act quickly to take advantage of the offer.

Transactional emails are triggered by a specific action taken by the recipient, such as making a purchase or signing up for a service. These emails often include order confirmations, shipping notifications, and password resets. For transactional emails, clarity and relevance are crucial. The subject line should clearly state the purpose of the email, such as "Your Order Confirmation" or "Your Package Has Shipped." While transactional emails typically have high open rates due to their nature, a clear and concise subject line ensures that the recipient knows exactly what to expect.

Informational emails provide valuable content to the recipient without necessarily promoting a product or service. These emails might include newsletters, blog updates, or educational content. For informational emails, the subject line should highlight the value of the content. Pique the reader's curiosity or promise a benefit, such as "5 Tips to Boost Your Productivity" or "How to Master Email Marketing." The goal is to make the recipient want to read the content because it offers something valuable to them.

Seasonal and event-based emails capitalize on specific times of the year or special occasions. These emails can create a sense of relevance and timeliness, encouraging recipients to engage. For seasonal emails, incorporating the season or holiday into the subject line can be effective, such as "Get Ready for Summer with Our New Collection" or "Holiday Sale: Save Big This Christmas." Event-based emails can highlight the importance of the event, such as "Join Us for Our Annual Conference" or "Don't Miss Our Webinar on Email Marketing Trends."

Tailoring your subject lines to fit the type of email you're sending is essential for maximizing their effectiveness. Understanding the purpose of each email and the mindset of your audience when they receive it can help you craft subject lines that resonate.

As we delve deeper into email subject lines, it's also important to consider the challenges you might face. From avoiding spam filters to staying creative and relevant, there are several obstacles that can impact the success of your subject lines. In the next chapter, we'll explore common challenges and provide strategies for overcoming them, ensuring that your subject lines continue to perform well and engage your audience.

# Chapter 7: Overcoming Common Challenges

———

Crafting effective email subject lines is not without its challenges. From avoiding spam filters to staying creative and relevant, there are several obstacles that can impact the success of your subject lines. In this chapter, we'll explore common challenges and provide strategies for overcoming them.

One of the biggest challenges in email marketing is avoiding spam filters. Spam filters are designed to protect recipients from unwanted and potentially harmful emails. However, they can sometimes flag legitimate emails as spam, preventing them from reaching the inbox. To avoid spam filters, it's important to follow best practices for email marketing. This includes avoiding spammy language and excessive punctuation in your subject lines, such as using all caps or multiple exclamation marks. It's also crucial to maintain a good sender reputation by regularly cleaning your email list and removing inactive or invalid email addresses.

Another challenge is staying creative and fresh with your subject lines. With so many emails flooding inboxes every day, it can be difficult to stand out. One way to stay creative is to keep a swipe file of subject lines that catch your attention. This can be a source of inspiration when you're feeling stuck. Additionally, brainstorming sessions with your team can generate new ideas and perspectives. Don't be afraid to experiment with different styles and approaches to see what resonates with your audience.

Relevance is another critical factor in the success of your subject lines. If your subject lines aren't relevant to your audience, they are less likely to be opened. To ensure relevance, it's important to segment your audience and tailor your subject lines to each segment's interests and needs. Personalization can also enhance relevance, making your emails feel more tailored and specific to the recipient.

Maintaining a balance between being intriguing and informative can also be challenging. A subject line that is too vague may not provide enough information to entice the recipient to open the email, while a subject line that is too detailed may give away too much and reduce curiosity. Striking the right balance requires understanding your audience and testing different approaches to see what works best.

Writer's block and idea fatigue are common challenges when crafting subject lines. When you're sending emails regularly, it can be difficult to come up with new and compelling subject lines. One strategy to overcome this is to repurpose successful subject lines from the past. If a subject line performed well before, consider tweaking it slightly to create a fresh variation. Additionally, staying updated on industry trends and keeping an eye on what your competitors are doing can provide new ideas and inspiration.

Finally, measuring the success of your subject lines and making data-driven decisions is crucial for continuous improvement. Tracking key metrics such as open rates, click-through rates, and conversion rates can provide valuable insights into what works and what doesn't. Regularly reviewing and analyzing these metrics can help you refine your approach and achieve better results over time.

Overcoming these challenges requires a combination of creativity, strategy, and continuous learning. By staying proactive and adaptable, you can ensure that your subject lines remain effective and engaging.

With a solid understanding of how to overcome common challenges, let's move on to leveraging data and trends to inform your subject line strategy. In the next chapter, we'll explore how to use data and stay ahead of trends to create subject lines that resonate with your audience and drive engagement.

# Chapter 8: Leveraging Data and Trends

In the fast-paced world of email marketing, leveraging data and staying ahead of trends can significantly enhance the effectiveness of your subject lines. Data provides valuable insights into your audience's behavior, while trends can inform your strategy and help you stay relevant. This chapter will explore how to use data and trends to create compelling subject lines that resonate with your audience.

Data is a powerful tool for informing your subject line strategy. By analyzing data from your past email campaigns, you can gain insights into what works and what doesn't. Key metrics to track include open rates, click-through rates (CTR), and conversion rates. Open rates indicate how many recipients opened your email, while CTR measures how many clicked on a link within the email. Conversion rates track how many recipients took the desired action, such as making a purchase or signing up for a webinar.

To leverage data effectively, start by identifying patterns and trends in your email performance. For example, you might notice that subject lines with a sense of urgency tend to have higher open rates, or that personalized subject lines result in more conversions. These insights can inform your future subject line strategy and help you create more effective emails.

In addition to analyzing your own data, it's also important to stay updated on industry trends. Trends can provide valuable insights into what's resonating with audiences and help you stay ahead of the curve. For example, you might notice that emojis are becoming popular in subject lines or that certain words and phrases are trending. Incorporating these trends into your subject lines can make your emails feel fresh and relevant.

There are several tools available that can help you analyze data and identify trends. Email marketing platforms often provide built-in analytics that track key metrics and generate reports. Additionally, tools like Google Trends can help you identify trending topics and keywords. Social media platforms are also valuable sources of trend data, as they can provide insights into what your audience is talking about and engaging with.

Once you've gathered data and identified trends, the next step is to apply these insights to your subject lines. For example, if your data shows that subject lines with a sense of urgency perform well, you might incorporate urgency into more of your subject lines. Similarly, if a certain keyword or phrase is trending, you might include it in your subject lines to capitalize on its popularity.

It's also important to test and refine your approach continuously. A/B testing different subject lines and analyzing the results can help you understand what resonates best with your audience. By regularly testing and refining your subject lines, you can ensure that they remain effective and engaging over time.

Staying ahead of trends and leveraging data is an ongoing process. The digital landscape is constantly evolving, and what works today might not work tomorrow. By staying proactive and adaptable, you can ensure that your subject lines continue to perform well and drive engagement.

With a solid understanding of how to leverage data and trends, let's explore advanced techniques and strategies for crafting subject lines. In the next chapter, we'll dive into using humor, storytelling, and multimedia to create subject lines that stand out and capture your audience's attention.

# Chapter 9: Advanced Techniques and Strategies

———

As we've explored the basics of crafting effective subject lines, leveraging psychological principles, and using data and trends, it's time to dive into advanced techniques and strategies. These approaches can help you create subject lines that stand out even more and capture your audience's attention. In this chapter, we'll explore using humor, storytelling, and multimedia in your subject lines.

Humor is a powerful tool for engaging your audience and making your emails memorable. A well-crafted humorous subject line can make your email stand out in a crowded inbox and encourage recipients to open it. For example, a subject line like "Why Did the Chicken Cross the Road? Find Out in Our Latest Newsletter" can pique curiosity and bring a smile to the reader's face. However, it's important to use humor appropriately and ensure it aligns with your brand's voice and tone. Not every audience will respond well to humor, so it's essential to know your audience and test different approaches.

Storytelling is another effective technique for crafting compelling subject lines. Humans are naturally drawn to stories, and a subject line that hints at a story can intrigue the reader and encourage them to open the email. For example, a subject line like "How One Small Change Transformed My Life" suggests a personal story that the reader will want to know more about. Using storytelling elements in your subject lines can create an emotional connection with your audience and make your emails more engaging.

Incorporating multimedia elements, such as emojis, can also enhance your subject lines. Emojis can add visual interest and convey emotions quickly, making your subject lines more engaging and eye-catching. For example, a subject line like "Get Ready for Summer ☀ New Collection Inside" uses the sun emoji to evoke a sense of summer fun. However, it's important to use emojis sparingly and ensure they are relevant to the content of your email. Overuse of emojis can make your emails look unprofessional and detract from your message.

Another advanced technique is mobile optimization. With the increasing use of smartphones, it's essential to ensure your subject lines are optimized for mobile devices. This means keeping them short and to the point, as longer subject lines may get cut off on smaller screens. Testing your subject lines on different devices can help you ensure they are fully visible and effective on all screens.

Personalization and targeting, as discussed in previous chapters, are also advanced strategies that can enhance your subject lines. By using dynamic content and segmentation, you can create highly tailored subject lines that resonate with specific groups of recipients. For example, a subject line like "Exclusive Offer for Our Best Customers" can make recipients feel valued and appreciated.

Another advanced strategy is to create a sense of exclusivity in your subject lines. People are naturally drawn to things that are exclusive or limited. Subject lines that emphasize exclusivity can create a sense of importance and urgency, encouraging recipients to open the email. For example, "VIP Access: Early Bird Tickets Available Now" suggests that the recipient is getting special treatment and access to something valuable.

Continuous learning and improvement are key to mastering advanced techniques. Staying updated on industry trends, experimenting with different approaches, and analyzing your results can help you refine your strategy and achieve better results over time. By continuously testing and refining your subject lines, you can ensure they remain effective and engaging.

As we wrap up our exploration of advanced techniques, it's time to build a sustainable strategy that keeps your audience engaged over the long term. In the next chapter, we'll discuss how to create a long-term plan for subject line success, including tips for continuous learning and improvement, building a toolkit of resources, and keeping your audience engaged.

# Chapter 10: Building a Sustainable Strategy

———

With a deep understanding of the techniques and strategies for crafting compelling email subject lines, it's time to build a sustainable strategy that keeps your audience engaged over the long term. This chapter will guide you through creating a long-term plan for subject line success, including tips for continuous learning and improvement, building a toolkit of resources, and keeping your audience engaged.

Creating a sustainable strategy starts with setting clear goals for your email marketing campaigns. Define what you want to achieve with your emails, whether it's increasing open rates, boosting click-through rates, or driving conversions. Having clear goals will guide your subject line strategy and help you measure your success.

Continuous learning and improvement are essential for maintaining the effectiveness of your subject lines. The digital landscape is constantly evolving, and what works today might not work tomorrow. Stay updated on industry trends, new techniques, and best practices by reading industry blogs, attending webinars, and participating in online communities. Regularly testing and analyzing your subject lines will provide valuable insights into what resonates with your audience and help you refine your approach.

Building a toolkit of resources can also support your long-term strategy. Keep a swipe file of successful subject lines that catch your attention. This can serve as a source of inspiration when you're feeling stuck. Additionally, create templates for different types of emails, such as promotional, transactional, and informational emails. These templates can provide a starting point for crafting new subject lines and ensure consistency in your email marketing efforts.

Keeping your audience engaged over time requires a deep understanding of their needs and preferences. Regularly survey your audience to gather feedback on your emails, including the subject lines. Use this feedback to inform your strategy and make adjustments as needed. Personalization and segmentation, as discussed in previous chapters, can also help keep your emails relevant and engaging.

Another important aspect of a sustainable strategy is maintaining a healthy email list. Regularly clean your email list by removing inactive or invalid email addresses. This will help improve your sender reputation and ensure your emails reach the inbox. Additionally, segmenting your list based on engagement levels can help you target your subject lines more effectively.

Consistency is key to building trust with your audience. Ensure that your subject lines align with your brand's voice and tone. Whether your brand is playful and fun or serious and professional, consistency in your subject lines will help create a cohesive experience for your audience. Additionally, be transparent and honest in your subject lines. Avoid misleading or clickbait subject lines that promise something the email doesn't deliver. This can damage your credibility and lead to lower open rates over time.

Staying creative and fresh is also essential for a sustainable strategy. Experiment with different styles and approaches to keep your subject lines interesting. This could include using humor, storytelling, and multimedia, as discussed in previous chapters. Don't be afraid to try new things and take risks. Testing different approaches will help you understand what resonates with your audience and keep your emails engaging.

Finally, remember that email marketing is a long-term game. Building a sustainable strategy requires patience, persistence, and continuous effort. By staying proactive, adaptable, and focused on your goals, you can create subject lines that not only get noticed but get opened.

With a solid foundation for a sustainable strategy, let's explore how automation and tools can help you streamline your email marketing efforts. In the next chapter, we'll discuss how to use automation to create efficient workflows and maintain personalization, ensuring your subject lines remain effective and engaging.

# Chapter 11: Automation and Tools for Efficiency

───

As email marketing continues to evolve, automation and tools play a crucial role in streamlining processes and enhancing efficiency. This chapter will explore how to use automation to create efficient workflows and maintain personalization, ensuring your subject lines remain effective and engaging.

Email marketing automation allows you to set up automated workflows that trigger emails based on specific actions or events. This can save you time and ensure your emails are sent at the optimal moment. For example, you can set up an automated welcome email that is sent to new subscribers as soon as they sign up. The subject line for this email could be something like "Welcome to Our Community, [Name]!" Personalizing the subject line with the recipient's name adds a personal touch and makes the email feel more relevant.

There are several tools available that can help you set up and manage automated workflows. Popular email marketing platforms like Mailchimp, HubSpot, and ActiveCampaign offer robust automation features that allow you to create complex workflows with ease. These tools often include drag-and-drop interfaces that make it easy to design and customize your automation sequences.

One of the key benefits of automation is the ability to maintain personalization at scale. With dynamic content and segmentation, you can create personalized subject lines for each recipient, even when sending emails to large lists. For example, you can use dynamic content to insert the recipient's name, location, or past purchase history into the subject line. This level of personalization can significantly increase open rates and engagement.

Automation also allows you to set up behavior-triggered emails that respond to specific actions taken by the recipient. For example, if a recipient abandons their shopping cart, you can send an automated email with a subject line like "Don't Forget! Complete Your Purchase Today." This type of email can help recover lost sales and keep your audience engaged.

In addition to automation, there are several tools available that can help you create and test your subject lines. Tools like CoSchedule's Headline Analyzer and Advanced Marketing Institute's Headline Analyzer can provide insights into the effectiveness of your subject lines, offering suggestions for improvement. These tools analyze factors such as word balance, emotional impact, and readability to help you craft compelling subject lines.

Another valuable tool for email marketers is the A/B testing feature offered by most email marketing platforms. A/B testing allows you to compare different subject lines and see which one performs better. This can help you understand what resonates with your audience and refine your approach for better results. Regularly testing your subject lines can provide valuable insights and ensure your emails remain effective over time.

While automation and tools can significantly enhance your email marketing efforts, it's important to use them wisely. Maintaining a balance between automation and personalization is crucial for creating a positive experience for your audience. Over-automation or relying too heavily on tools can make your emails feel impersonal and robotic. It's essential to keep the human touch and ensure your emails reflect your brand's voice and values.

With automation and tools, you can streamline your email marketing processes and maintain personalization at scale. However, it's also important to consider the unique challenges and opportunities in different industries. In the next chapter, we'll explore industry-specific strategies for crafting effective subject lines and learn from case studies of successful campaigns.

# Chapter 12: Industry-Specific Strategies

———

Email marketing strategies can vary significantly across different industries, each with its unique challenges and opportunities. In this chapter, we'll explore industry-specific strategies for crafting effective subject lines and learn from case studies of successful campaigns.

Different industries have different audiences, goals, and competitive landscapes, which can influence the effectiveness of email subject lines. For example, the e-commerce industry often focuses on driving sales and promoting products. Subject lines in this industry might emphasize discounts, new arrivals, and limited-time offers. An effective subject line for an e-commerce email could be "Flash Sale: 50% Off All Items Today Only!" This creates a sense of urgency and highlights the value of the offer.

In the B2B (business-to-business) sector, the focus is often on building relationships and providing valuable information. Subject lines in this industry might emphasize industry insights, case studies, and educational content. An effective subject line for a B2B email could be "Discover the Latest Trends in Digital Marketing." This promises valuable information that can help the recipient stay ahead of the curve in their industry.

Non-profits and charities often use email marketing to engage supporters and drive donations. Subject lines in this industry might emphasize the impact of donations, upcoming events, and success stories. An effective subject line for a non-profit email could be "Your Support Changed a Life – Read Their Story." This creates an emotional connection and highlights the positive impact of the recipient's support.

Case studies from various industries can provide valuable insights into effective email marketing strategies. For example, a case study from an e-commerce brand might show how personalized subject lines increased open rates and sales. Another case study from a B2B company might demonstrate how educational content in subject lines drove engagement and lead generation. These real-world examples can offer practical tips and inspiration for your own email marketing efforts.

Tailoring subject lines to fit the specific needs and preferences of your audience is crucial for maximizing their effectiveness. This might involve using industry-specific language, highlighting relevant benefits, and addressing common pain points. For example, in the travel industry, subject lines that emphasize exclusive deals, destination highlights, and travel tips can resonate well with the audience. An effective subject line for a travel email could be "Escape to Paradise: Exclusive Deals on Beach Vacations."

Learning from industry leaders can also provide valuable insights into effective email marketing strategies. Analyzing the subject lines of successful brands in your industry can help you understand what works and why. For example, if you notice that a leading competitor consistently uses a certain style or approach in their subject lines, you might experiment with similar techniques to see if they work for your audience.

Cross-industry insights and best practices can also inform your subject line strategy. While different industries have unique challenges and opportunities, there are common principles that apply across the board. These include creating a sense of urgency, sparking curiosity, and personalizing your subject lines. By combining industry-specific strategies with cross-industry best practices, you can create subject lines that resonate with your audience and drive engagement.

As we wrap up our exploration of industry-specific strategies, it's important to consider the future of email subject lines. Emerging trends and technologies, such as AI and machine learning, are set to revolutionize email marketing. In the next chapter, we'll explore the future of email subject lines and how you can stay ahead of the curve.

# Chapter 13: The Future of Email Subject Lines

———

The world of email marketing is constantly evolving, and staying ahead of the curve is essential for maintaining the effectiveness of your subject lines. In this chapter, we'll explore the future of email subject lines, including emerging trends and technologies that are set to revolutionize email marketing.

One of the most significant trends shaping the future of email marketing is the rise of artificial intelligence (AI) and machine learning. These technologies are transforming how marketers create and optimize subject lines. AI can analyze vast amounts of data to identify patterns and trends that can inform your subject line strategy. For example, AI-powered tools can predict which subject lines are likely to perform best based on past performance and real-time data.

Machine learning algorithms can also personalize subject lines at scale, making it possible to tailor each subject line to the individual recipient. This level of personalization can significantly increase open rates and engagement. For example, an AI-powered tool might analyze a recipient's past behavior and preferences to generate a personalized subject line like "John, Discover New Adventures in Your Area."

Another emerging trend is the use of predictive analytics to forecast recipient behavior. Predictive analytics can help you understand how likely recipients are to open your emails based on various factors, such as their past engagement and demographic information. This can inform your subject line strategy and help you create subject lines that resonate with your audience.

Voice search is another trend that is set to impact email marketing. As more people use voice assistants like Siri, Alexa, and Google Assistant, optimizing your subject lines for voice search can help you stay ahead of the curve. This involves using natural language and conversational tones in your subject lines. For example, a subject line like "What's New in Your Area?" can be more effective for voice search than a more formal subject line.

Interactive content is also gaining traction in email marketing. Subject lines that hint at interactive elements, such as polls, quizzes, or videos, can drive higher engagement. For example, a subject line like "Take Our Quick Quiz and Win a Prize!" can encourage recipients to open the email and participate in the interactive content.

Personalization and segmentation will continue to play a crucial role in the future of email marketing. As technology advances, the ability to collect and analyze data will improve, making it easier to create highly personalized subject lines. This includes using dynamic content, behavior-triggered emails, and real-time data to tailor subject lines to each recipient.

The increasing focus on privacy and data protection is another factor that will shape the future of email marketing. With regulations like the General Data Protection Regulation (GDPR) and the California Consumer Privacy Act (CCPA), it's essential to ensure your email marketing practices comply with these regulations. This includes being transparent about how you collect and use data and ensuring recipients have the option to opt-out of emails.

Preparing for the future of email subject lines involves staying updated on emerging trends and technologies, continuously testing and refining your approach, and being adaptable to change. By leveraging the power of AI, predictive analytics, and interactive content, you can create subject lines that resonate with your audience and drive engagement.

As we wrap up our journey through the world of email subject lines, it's important to remember that mastering email marketing is an ongoing process. The digital landscape is constantly evolving, and staying ahead requires continuous learning and improvement. By applying the principles and strategies discussed in this book, you can create subject lines that not only get noticed but get opened.

Thank you for joining me on this journey. I wish you great success in your email marketing endeavors. Now, go forth and craft those perfect subject lines!